Twenty Blues

J.D Revels

BookLeaf Publishing

India | USA | UK

Presentation by *BookLeaf Publishing*

Web: www.bookleafpub.com

E-mail: info@bookleafpub.com

ISBN: 9789363307995

First edition 2024

*To all the dreamers, readers, and writers...the
world needs more of you*

ACKNOWLEDGEMENT

Wow. What a joy it is that I am able to write poetry and have an outlet for any sort of idea that pops up. I am so grateful that I found a love for this, and it wouldn't be possible without the one person that introduced me to it in the first place. Rachel, you are the sister I never got to have. You have changed my life in all the best ways and have been a shoulder to cry on through all the tough years. I will cherish every 2 AM gas station deep chat we have ever shared and will continue to share in the future. Thank you for always sharing your beautiful work and for inspiring me to create my own. I would also like to acknowledge my wonderful loving family, for always supporting me wherever I go. I never thought that life outside of college would lead me to this point, yet I can't imagine it any other way. You all are the best, and I love you. And to you, dear reader, thank you for taking the time to dive into my ramblings. I hope it was inspiring to you in some way. Go on, be a dreamer, and never stop writing! Xo

PREFACE

First of all, I want to say...hi! I am so glad you are here. If you did pick up this book, you are most likely a young adult who may be feeling a little lost in life in some way or another. Plus, you picked up a poetry book, so that means you are officially super cool because poetry is awesome! No matter where you are in life right now, I want you to know that at the end of the day, it is okay to anything you are feeling right now. You are not lost, you are young and finding your own way in this great wide world. Each day we learn something new about ourselves or come face to face with a new emotion from a current phase of life. Face it, feel it, and if you want to…write about it. Express your own art and don't feel pressure to be like everyone else. Writing poetry is art and expression, it's messy and though it is lyrical and tells a story in a few words, it is poignant. I have always thought that poetry is like journaling but with more feeling (and of course fewer words). And what is special about it is it can be relative to the reader in a completely opposite way than its original intention. And something about that is beautiful. It's as if the words are a living and breathing piece of something that changes each time you read it. So my hope for you, dear reader and lover of this art, is that you may be moved in some way by these collections. I hope you feel seen. Twenty-somethings are full of growing pains, but there is much beauty in it.

If they say with time a deep wound heals
Why does it feel like mine remains?
Though it may not be agonizing any longer
In some ways it is still a part of me
A part that only I can see
And I wonder if I am really just afraid to give it
up

Losing a love that was real
I think takes away more than a person can
realize
You can't notice it
Until the idea of pursuance exists again
And somewhere in the realm of infinite
possibility
Of infinite choice
You feel different
As if the weight of the pieces of you that are no
longer
Grow heavier in their absence
But you have to learn to live without them

First it came in swells
The feeling of deep loss
Now resigned to ripples of loneliness
Reminding me that what I desire most
Is to be chosen
To one day be the one found in a crowded room
And feel everything else fade away under the
weight of a lovers gaze
One day, I tell myself
And I dream in the maybes
Without actually believing it
A hopeless romantic trapped in the shell of
indifference

It's not commitment to a new someone that
keeps me two steps away
This heart I wear on my sleeve is ready to be
claimed
But rather it's looking into the glossy eyes of
another again in the end
And knowing before they even say a word
That it's over
It's a special kind of torture in that moment
Realizing everything
Every word
Was not enough to make them stay

The other side of grief is a peculiar thing
You can overcome mountains built with it
Standing with pride at the you now
The you that is new and whole
But yet still wish you could see them one last
time
To feel a sort of sadness at the thought that the
last memory shared
Was of two souls broken apart
It's as if you could have one last wish
To look into the eyes of the one you thought was
forever
And say, thank you, I have found me again
I am not where you left me
And I have come alive again
Yet still, I dream of meeting you again
Stranger

It's a sort of dread in the moment that you
realize
That what was once in your control is no longer
Plans unraveled
A blank slate to start again
One would think this freedom would feel
different
Limitless
Instead I feel trapped
The weight of disappointment heavy
For what could have been

No one tells you how tiring the search is
For your purpose, for that thing that is calling
you
Has always called you
But it's utterly exhausting sometimes
The push and pull
Of wanting but fearing
What the future holds
So I close my eyes
In and out I breathe
Day after day
Because betraying the idea of something more
Is betraying myself

Some days I want to be alone
Most days I think I am better off with just me
I find peace in solitude
In taking myself to the park and reading under
the sun
In long car drives with music that speaks to the
soul
I long to visit faraway places where beauty is
abundant
I dream of them
But sometimes I wonder if peace can be found in
solitude forever
Or is it all temporary
I fear what being alone will make of me

We reach so hard for purpose
For something that defines us
Sets us apart
I try so hard
Why does it seem then
That the more I try to search for it
The more I get the feeling
That I am running away from something
But chasing nothing

</p>

Time confuses me more than ever
Thinking in years makes time appear too fast
Yet in days it seems abundant
So much time yet none at all
Somehow childhood feels closer
Than the end of youth
How must I not take it for granted?
I think about it often
And it scares me most days

It's funny when you grow older
How certain people you meet just seem different
Like an unspoken connection
Although they are strangers, some are familiar
As if their face holds a faint memory
In some other walk of life forgotten

The things that seemed important before
Have drifted away with the passing wind
I want to run in the direction of adventure
Where the soul can be free
Knowing no limits
And embracing what is unknown

Fleeting moments of life are often clung to
Some hold on for dear life
Others let their grip give out
Slowly, gently, almost without notice
Until now is traded with then
It's a passing of you for another
And you are not the same
How could it be
Just as a stream billows down a mountain
Passing over rocks and weathering its path
Gravity demanding its journey never stop
A constant flow of change
So too are we strangers to complacency
And there is a certain beauty in the inevitability
Of time demanding the same of us

Most days I can't seem to clear my head
I scroll and I swipe through a thousand lives
A thousand lives to dream of in my head
But it doesn't seem to help
So I write and I ramble
To make sense of it all
To give my sensibilities a home
And somewhere amidst it all
I'm learning to make friends with it
Of being lost

Let me be anything in the world
Except the one person
Who steps in my way
Who stops me from entertaining possibility
After all
It is only me who can choose
Let me stay young at heart

Aceptar la transformación
Es aceptar la contradicción de ti mismo
- ROSALÍA

To accept transformation
Is to accept the contradiction of yourself
- ROSALÍA

What a privilege it is to know that
I am able to feel
To feel glorious and euphoric
Joy and wonder at beautiful things
And to feel grief
Heartbreak and loneliness
The throbbing pain of loss
I am able to feel
When emotions swell over my head
I remind myself of this
To be grateful that I am here
That the swells from the past weren't enough to
break me
I can feel

There's something there
A whisper
A faint lull in the distance
Only heard in the silence
In the absence of the noise
Telling me that there's more
There's something more out there
So I walk toward it
Hoping I find it somewhere
Hoping it finds me soon

I think about the concept of life a lot
About the seasons
The highs and lows that no one knows about
I think about how extraordinary it is
That a different form of me exists with each one
along the way
With each season I meet someone new
I look in the mirror into the eyes of a version of
me
And I smile at her
A soft hello as a greeting
She looks at me back
And waves her hand in goodbye
Because someone new will take her place

Darling,
Don't you know that
It's okay to stay
To leave
To come back
And to never return
Spread your arms out wide to the wind
To what is
What you can be
And follow what calls your name

I look forward to noticing small things these
days
Vibrance of colors in the sky as the sun lays
itself to rest
The glittering ripples of water on a glassy lake
The sound of aspens rustling in the wind
Like distant ocean waves
I notice there is power to taking notes of beauty
To relish in simple joy of being alive
Because oh, how futile it all is